MY FIRST LOOK AT PLANETS

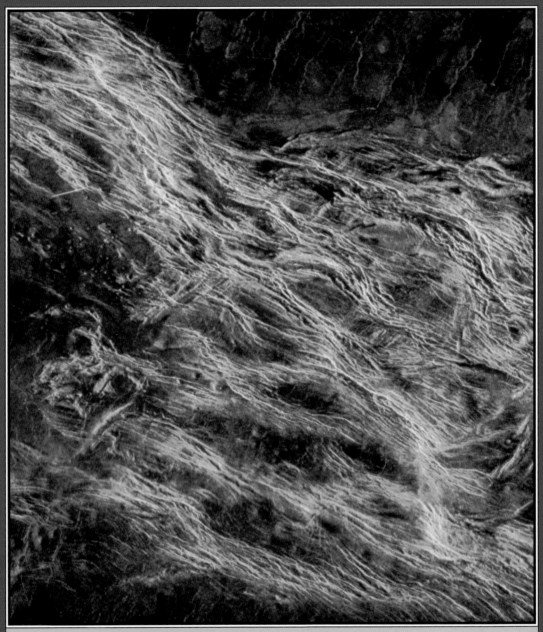

VENUS'S SURFACE IS LIKE A HOT, DRY DESERT

Venus

TERESA WIMMER

CREATIVE EDUCATION

Published by Creative Education

P.O. Box 227, Mankato, Minnesota 56002

Creative Education is an imprint of The Creative Company

Designed by Rita Marshall

Photographs by Getty Images (Stone), Tom Stack & Associates (JPL, NASA, TSADO)

Copyright © 2008 Creative Education

Printed in the United States of America

Library of Congress Cataloging-in-Publication Data

Wimmer, Teresa, 1975- Venus / by Teresa Wimmer.

p. cm. — (My first look at planets)

Includes index.

ISBN-13: 978-1-58341-524-5

1. Venus (Planet)—Juvenile literature. I. Title.

QB621.W56 2007   523.42—dc22   2006018254

First edition 9 8 7 6 5 4 3 2 1

VENUS

WHITE AND BRIGHT

A long time ago, people saw a bright light in the sky. It was there just before the sun rose and after the sun went down. People called the light the "morning star" and the "evening star." But the light was not a star. It was the **planet** Venus.

Venus is close to Earth, so it is easy to see in the sky. White clouds cover Venus. They

VENUS SHARES THE SKY WITH MILLIONS OF STARS

make it look bright and pretty. Some people call Venus the "jewel of the sky."

Venus is about the same size as Earth. A long time ago, people thought Venus was like Earth. But Venus is not like any other planet.

Venus is the only planet
people on Earth can see
during the daytime.

Hot Spinner

Venus is part of the **solar system**. Besides Venus, there are seven other planets. All of the planets move in an **orbit** around the sun. Venus is the second planet from the sun.

Like all planets, Venus spins like a top. It never stops spinning. Only one side of Venus faces the sun at a time. That side has daytime. The side that faces away from the sun has nighttime.

Most of the planets spin

the same way. But Venus

spins the other way.

Heat from the sun makes Venus the hottest planet of all. The clouds on Venus are very thick. They trap the sun's heat. Walking on Venus would be like walking on fire!

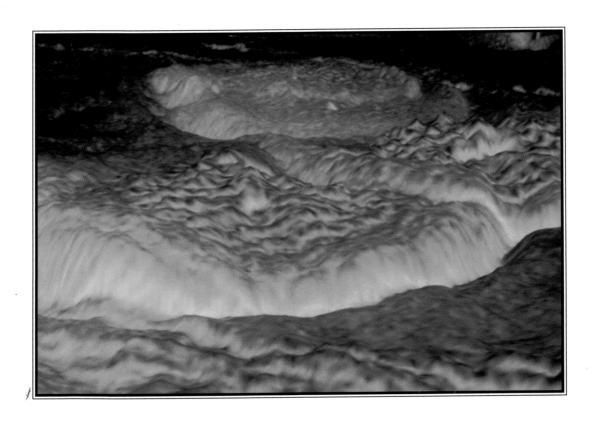

Some people think there

was once water on Venus.

The heat made it dry up.

No Life

Venus is a big ball of rock. There are flat lands on Venus. There are hot mountains called volcanoes, too.

The volcanoes push out hot, melted rock called lava. Lava covers most of Venus's ground. There are no lakes or rivers on Venus. It never rains there.

VOLCANOES HAVE HELPED SHAPE VENUS'S SURFACE

No people live on Venus. No animals or plants live there, either. It is too hot. There is no fresh air to breathe. The clouds on Venus are filled with a harmful **gas**. People would die if they breathed the gas.

More to Learn

People have seen Venus for a long time. But it is hard to see through Venus's clouds. There is still a lot that people do not know about it.

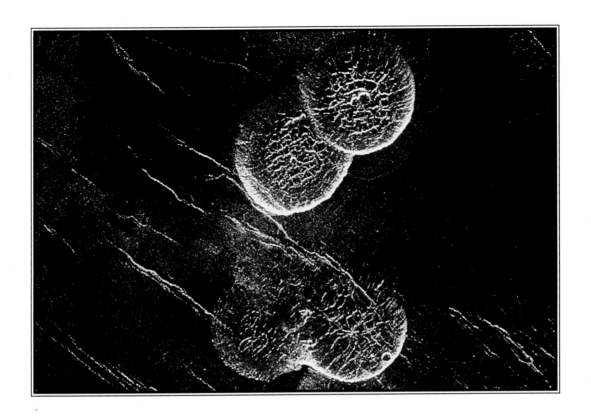

One day on Venus is
almost as long as a
whole year on Earth!

COOLED LAVA FORMS LARGE HILLS ON VENUS

VENUS HAS MANY HUGE HOLES CALLED CRATERS

To see Venus better, people send **probes** there. The probes carry special cameras. The cameras take pictures of Venus. The pictures get sent back to people on Earth. They show what Venus looks like under the clouds.

More probes will be sent to Venus soon. They will send new pictures back to people. Looking at the pictures will help people learn more about Venus!

THE *MAGELLAN* PROBE FLEW FROM EARTH TO VENUS

Hands-on: Make a Planet Venus

Up close, Venus is a white, pretty planet. You can make your very own planet Venus!

What You Need

A medium Styrofoam ball

20 small, white cotton balls

A piece of yarn about eight
   inches (20 cm) long

An orange marker

Glue

What You Do

1. Color thick, orange swirls (lava) all over the Styrofoam ball.
2. Glue the cotton balls on the Styrofoam ball.
3. Glue one end of the yarn to the top of the ball.
4. Now you have your own planet Venus. Hold on to the top of the yarn. Make Venus spin!

PROBES HAVE MADE MAPS OF VENUS'S SURFACE

INDEX

WORDS TO KNOW

gas—a kind of air; some gases are harmful to breathe

orbit—the path a planet takes around the sun or a moon takes around a planet

planet—a round object that moves around the sun

probes—special machines that fly around or land on a planet or a moon

solar system—the sun, the planets, and their moons

READ MORE

Chrismer, Melanie. *Venus.* New York: Scholastic, 2005.

Rudy, Lisa Jo. *Planets!* New York: HarperCollins, 2005.

Vogt, Gregory. *Solar System.* New York: Scholastic, 2001.

EXPLORE THE WEB

Enchanted Learning: Venus http://www.zoomschool.com/subjects/astronomy/planets/venus

Funschool: Space http://funschool.kaboose.com/globe-rider/space/index.html?trnstl=1

StarChild: The Planet Venus http://starchild.gsfc.nasa.gov/docs/StarChild/solar_system_level1/venus.html